Things
to
See

Things to See

a child's world of familiar objects

PHOTOGRAPHED IN COLOR
BY THOMAS MATTHIESEN

PLATT & MUNK, *Publishers* / NEW YORK
A Division of Grosset & Dunlap

Published by Platt & Munk, 1968.
All rights reserved.
Library of Congress Catalog Card No.:
66-13381
ISBN 0-448-41051-6
Printed in the United States of America

ball

Balls are always round so they can bounce and roll. A square ball wouldn't be any fun, would it?

brush and comb

A brush and comb keep your hair neat.
People who live in windy places use them often.

blocks

Blocks are wooden cubes that often have letters on them. Can you spell your name with your blocks?

fish

Fish live in the water and they like it very much.
That is why they are so hard to catch.

orange

An orange is wonderful to start off the day with, because it tastes full of sunshine.

stairs

Stairs let you go up or come down,
depending on where you start from.

blackboard

A blackboard is like a magic thing.
When you rub off what's written on it,
it gets all black again.

truck

Trucks can take heavy things like sand and coal over long distances without getting tired the way a man would.

crayons

Crayons let you write or draw in different colors. A red crayon will never make a blue line. Do you know why?

tree

Some trees grow very tall. Have you ever
looked up and seen the top of a tall tree
dancing in the wind?

cat

Cats like cream, warm places to sleep, and being clean. A cat always knows when its face needs washing.

trumpet

A trumpet makes a very loud noise.
Never blow one when people are sleeping.
They will be angry when they wake up.

ocean

Oceans take up the space between all the lands of the world. An ocean is so wide no one can see all the way across it.

scissors

With scissors you can cut paper and cloth into things like houses, flowers, animals and people. Have you ever tried?

butterfly

Butterflies go around from one pretty flower
to another, which is a very pleasant way
to spend a day.

candle

Candles have been used for thousands of years. Before the electric light was invented, people read books by candlelight.

tricycle

A tricycle always has three wheels and this makes it much easier to ride than a bicycle.

boat

Boats carry people and things across the water. The secret of a boat is that it floats. Do you know why?

marbles

Marbles are round and made of glass.
One marble is fun, but 14 marbles
are much better.

chair

Chairs are made for people to sit in.
When you are tired, sitting in a chair
is much nicer than standing.

dog

A dog is a friendly animal and very good to have around if you want a ball chased or a bone buried.

cup

A cup is a good thing to drink from because it has a handle you can hold.

parrot

Parrots are birds that can be taught to speak like people. But even the smartest parrot doesn't have very much to say.

spoon

A spoon is very useful for eating certain foods. Soup, for instance, can't be eaten with a fork.

cookies

Cookies taste very good all by themselves,
but they are even better with a glass of milk.

zebra

Zebras have wonderful black and white stripes. Other animals would probably be very happy to look like a zebra.